13

A WRIGLEY BOOK
about

SPRINGS

BY DENIS WRIGLEY

Some metal will bend.

Some metal will snap if you bend it

but some metal won't stay bent. It will spring back if you let go!

The more we bend it the more it will try to unwind -
we have made a spring.

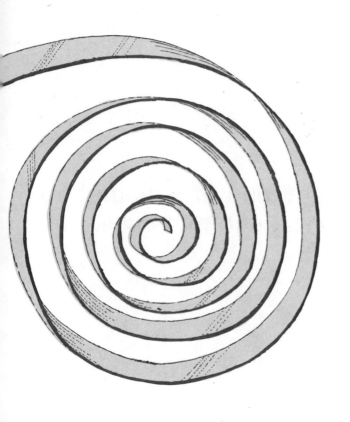

We can fix one end of a wound up spring so that it cannot move

but the loose end will still try to
unwind . . . .

We can make use of the unwinding of the spring if we fasten the loose end to a rod . . . .

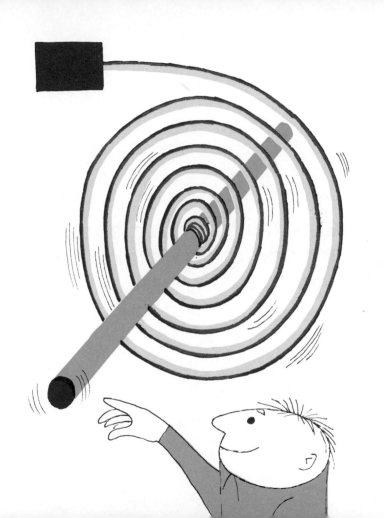

If the rod is held at both ends the unwinding spring will make the rod turn too.

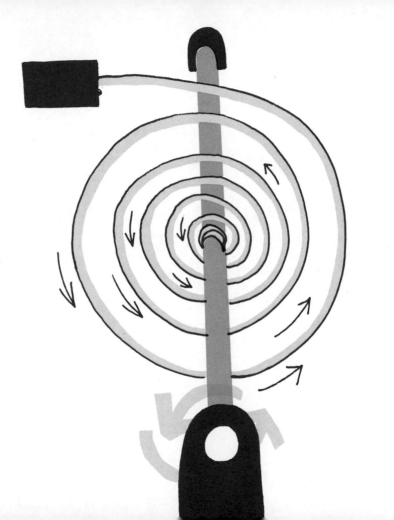

In this way the power of springs
can be made to turn rods
and wheels in toys
and clocks and things.

Another kind of spring is used for pushing and pulling.

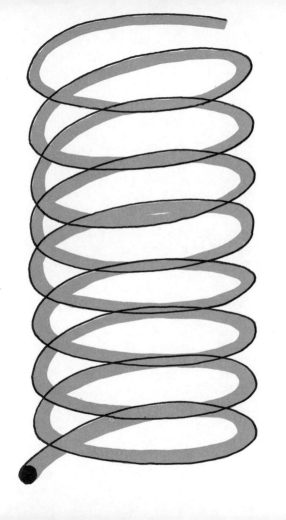

If we push it down . . . .

it will jump up again . . . .
A spring always tries to return to
the shape it was before it was bent
or pressed down - or pulled out.

We use these springs in chairs
and beds to support our weight

and in cars and mousetraps too!

When a spring is pulled and pulled
and pulled out until it's too
hard to pull any more, then

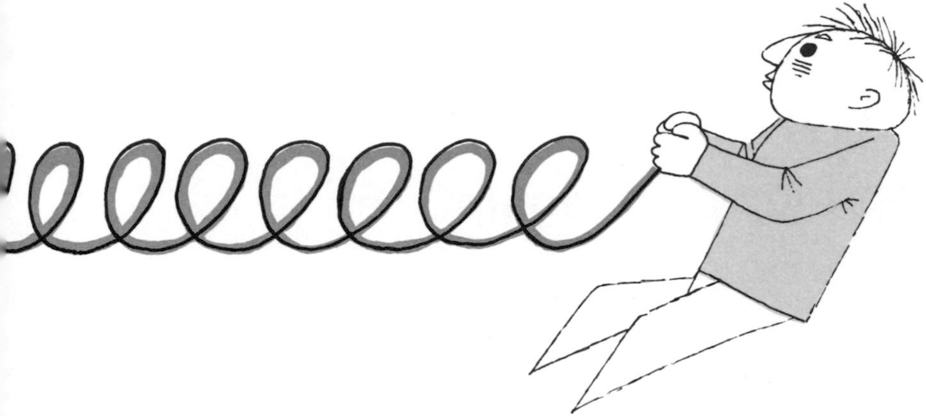

it springs back again!

This kind of spring can close doors and we can use it in bicycles and many things.

Look out . . . .

for springs - everywhere ! !

First published 1974
Copyright © 1974 Denis Wrigley
ISBN 0 7188 2095 9
Printed in Great Britain by
Redwood Press Limited
Trowbridge, Wiltshire

The Wrigley Books

Published by
LUTTERWORTH PRESS · GUILDFORD AND LONDON